Millennium Shakespeare

THE MERRY WIVES OF WINDSOR

MILLENNIUM SHAKESPEARE
Copyright © 2006 Michael J. Stewart and the Wine Dark Press Ltd.

ISBN 0-9536004-0-8

First published in Great Britain in 2006
by the Wine Dark Press Ltd.
Printed in Asia.

For other titles available in the series, visit
www.millenniumshakespeare.com

Author Michael J. Stewart
Preface by Professor Stanley Stewart
Edited by Jeffrey Kahan, Ph.D.
Adapted from *The Merry Wives of Windsor* by William Shakespeare

Designed by Fiona Raven
Copy editor Lorraine Roche
Illustrations by Lesley Buckingham
Trademarks and calligraphy by Peter Horridge

THE MERRY WIVES OF WINDSOR

Adapted by Michael J. Stewart

Preface by Professor Stanley Stewart

Edited by Jeffrey Kahan, Ph.D.

Illustrations by Lesley Buckingham

Illustrations

1. I am Sir John Falstaff   11
2. There is money; spend it, spend it; spend more   19
3. So throwing him in the water will do him benefit   27
4. I like it not when a woman has a great beard   33
5. We will do it: let him be sent for tomorrow   37
6. I am here a Windsor stag   41

PREFACE

Almost two hundred years ago, with a mind to introduce children to 'the beautiful English tongue' of the most celebrated author in the language, Charles Lamb and his sister Mary published *Tales from Shakespeare*. They meant their 'foretastes of the great pleasure' of Shakespeare to prepare young people for a lifelong appreciation of his plays. Since children found Shakespeare's language difficult, the *Tales* presented the events in simplified narrative form, while retaining some of the grandeur of blank verse. Because of their complexity, some of the plots needed to be simplified, too. Thinking the names and circumstances in the history plays often confusingly similar, the Lambs left them out entirely.

It did not take long for publishers to illustrate *Tales from Shakespeare*. In 1878, for instance, twelve photographs were used from the Boydell Gallery, including one used as a frontispiece, and were equally divided between comedies and tragedies. Later, Arthur Rackham's illustrations of *Tales from Shakespeare* were especially beautiful. Since the Lambs, there have been various attempts to bring the works of Shakespeare to children; many of them, *The Children's Shakespeare*, for instance, adorned with elegant illustrations.

Michael Stewart's *Millennium Shakespeare* is in this grand tradition, designed to attract young readers, not only by introducing them to the heightened language of Shakespeare, but also by encouraging their imagination with splendid visual representations of the subject matter. However, unlike *Tales from Shakespeare* and most of the successive volumes designed to introduce children to the works of England's greatest poet, *Millennium Shakespeare* presents comprehensive narrative treatment of the entire Shakespeare canon.

Two hundred years had passed from Shakespeare's time to that of the Lambs; and now another two hundred have gone by since that first attempt to interest and to educate young readers in the colossal scope and splendid diction of Shakespeare's plays. Stylistic changes have occurred in publishing, set design, directing and acting. Shakespeare's audience today is very different from the motley crowd that thronged into the Globe Theatre in the late-sixteenth and early seventeenth centuries. Therefore, no purpose would be served by separating our sense of Shakespearean drama from popular cinematic performances of such plays as *Twelfth Night, A Midsummer Night's Dream, Henry V, Romeo and Juliet, Hamlet, Othello, King Lear* and *Macbeth,* to mention but a few. Actors like John Barrymore, Laurence Olivier, Judith Anderson, Kenneth Branagh, Gwyneth Paltrow and Derek Jacobi – to say nothing of the notable directors and costume and set designers – have had as much influence in shaping the popular imagination of notable scenes and characters from Shakespeare's

plays, as have the sketches and paintings of such artists as John Everett Millais, William Holman Hunt and Arthur Rackham. Perhaps even more important in that respect are the hundreds of films that have been produced based on Shakespeare's works. Indeed, it could be argued that William Shakespeare from Stratford upon Avon, who may never have ventured further from the village of his birth than London, is the most successful screenwriter in history. Many youngsters who have never seen a Shakespeare play on stage have seen *Romeo and Juliet* on film.

From the early seventeenth century to the beginning of the third millennium, Shakespeare's literary reputation has flourished. But the competition for the attention of children, who – experts tell us – are all too often 'reluctant readers', is intense. We don't need to be hysterical defenders of a canon inscribed in stone to want the next generation of students to know Shakespeare; but that knowledge must begin somewhere. If an introduction to Shakespeare is to be successful, it is unlikely to be in the setting of an academic symposium. Rather, children need a vehicle like *Millennium Shakespeare* to prepare them for the adult experience of discovering the work of what many consider the most gifted writer who ever lived.

Stanley Stewart
Distinguished Professor of English
University of California, Riverside, CA, USA

FOREWORD

'All the world's a stage', Shakespeare wrote in *As You Like It*. We are all connected to and belong to this 'globe'; thrust upon it, no matter where we're from, no matter what our religion, faith or ideology. To share in something beautiful often inspires and illuminates the mind and spirit.

I first discovered Shakespeare during my twenties – rather late for the introduction of such a rich language – yet a new world opened up for me, enabling me to discover and to experience not only new feelings and emotions that were previously unknown to me, but also a world of literary revelations. I have since continued my endless and fascinating journey through the literary and creative world. But it was from that moment, some twenty years ago, that I dreamed of bringing my experience of Shakespeare to everyone.

For many, it is difficult to understand Shakespeare in its original form. Often, readers get no further than the first few lines of text. Sadly, for many other potential readers of Shakespeare, the curtain closes even before it has opened. When I first read Shakespeare, I was immediately drawn to the rhythm, the poetry, the emotion and vast knowledge that Shakespeare's work held within its pages. It was as though a door had opened and a light

had been switched on, allowing me to see through the darkness something exquisite, something that had always been there, yet for others remains hidden from view.

I realised that by combining beautiful language with magnificent art, I could open the door and switch on the light for many readers who might otherwise never discover Shakespeare. If I could manage to bring together artists from around the world – each artist offering an expression of their interpretation of these masterpieces – and combine their work with all of Shakespeare's canon, a whole new generation of readers might be motivated to further investigate the world of Shakespeare. My hope is that the easy-to-read *Millennium Shakespeare* series will educate, stimulate, develop and open the senses for all those who discover it, transporting the reader from this stage into a 'new world'.

I would like to give special thanks to my wonderful daughter Jessica, who has – almost since the day she was born – always been aware of my desire to bring *Millennium Shakespeare* to life. As she has grown into a young woman, I'm sure Jessica has at times wondered whether this series would ever come to print. And now, at last, we begin.

I would also like to thank my family and close friends for their unwavering support and patience in understanding my desire to bring Shakespeare to the modern world.

I would like to thank my editor, Associate Professor Jeffrey Kahan (University of La Verne), whose support has been invaluable during

the development of *Millennium Shakespeare*. I would also like to thank Professor of English Stanley Stewart, Riverside, California for his acknowledgment of the series, as well as copy editor Lorraine Roche, who has worked with great enthusiasm and energy on this project, and Canadian designer Fiona Raven for her continued efforts in developing this special series.

My thanks go, too, to all the artists who have contributed to the series, and to their associates who have continued to support my endeavours. My thanks extend to those few, those happy few, who always believed in this cultural vision – to bring to life the most beautiful and definitive series of Shakespeare's classic stories for modern readers throughout the world.

Michael J. Stewart, *Author*

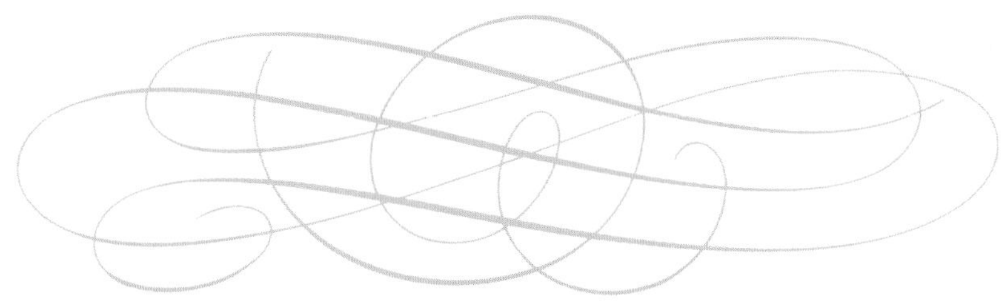

Falstaff

No quips now, Pistol. Indeed, I am in the waist two yards about. But I am now about no waste; I am about thrift. Briefly, I do mean to make love to Ford's wife. I spy entertainment in her. She discourses, she carves, she gives the leer of invitation. I can construe the action of her familiar style; and the hardest voice of her behaviour, to be Englished rightly, is, 'I am Sir John Falstaff's'.

THE MERRY WIVES OF WINDSOR

ituated in Windsor was an alehouse by the name of the Garter Inn. Friends and acquaintances would meet at this rather old inn to eat, drink and gossip. Though it was a noisy atmosphere, the inn was filled with jollity, laughter, plenty of sack beer and serving wenches.

Most people around the town knew of the infamous Sir John Falstaff, who had recently taken up residence at the Garter Inn. The truth is he often stayed here and, to him, it was like a home. He was known for his huge belly, which burst out from under his shirt and seemed to rest on his belt, or anything else in its way.

Falstaff was always coming up with bright ideas, although more often than not they never came to much. With a rosy face, he seemed larger than life, always jovial, happy and ready with a joke. He often had a tale to tell and was the life and soul of any party, or so he thought. If he wasn't laughing about something, others were laughing at him. But nothing was more pleasing to him than a large jug of wine to quench his great thirst and he never failed to accept a drink should anyone offer to buy one.

He boasted of his supposed conquests, glory, wealth and fortune. His name preceded him, but he was really a rascal and a rogue. He did have some friends and followers, who were

ever-ready to take advantage of some unsuspecting soul. They went by the names of Bardolph, Pistol and Nim.

Enter Justice Shallow, Master Slender and Sir Hugh Evans

Robert Shallow, the local justice, Sir Hugh Evans, the Welsh vicar, and Master Abraham Slender, a friend, were on their way to the Garter Inn to find Falstaff. They were musing over a certain Mistress Anne Page, the beautiful young daughter of a very wealthy and respected couple.

Slender had heard of this pretty young lady but had not met her. 'I know the young gentlewoman. She is well provided for.' Anne had recently received an inheritance from her grandparents, a rather large sum of money for those times, and everyone was talking about her.

For a moment, Shallow and Evans considered what Slender had said, and a thought suddenly struck Master Shallow. He

talked to Evans about it, and then they both began to think of a way for Slender to get to know Mistress Anne Page so that he could woo her.

Master Shallow also had a slightly more serious subject to discuss: Falstaff and his cronies had been poaching his deer, had beaten up the groundskeeper and broken into his lodge.

Enter Sir John

Naturally, Falstaff, being so full of himself – and of sack too – refused to accept or deny the accusation, even to the point of making fun of Master Shallow. In his usual witty way, Falstaff joked about the event.

Master Slender sets eyes on Mistress Page

'O heaven, this is Mistress Anne Page?' exclaimed Slender as she entered the room. Anne's father Mr Page suggested that they retire to have a drink.

Taking Slender to one side, Shallow inquired, 'Can you love the maid?'

'If you say "Marry her," I will marry her,' proffered Slender.

A follower rather than a leader, Slender agreed that he could love her indeed, if they wanted him to, and that if there were no great love in the beginning, certainly after they were married they would find love.

All was set and Master Shallow and Evans continued to make their plans to arrange a marriage between Slender and Mistress Anne Page.

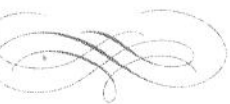

Dinner at Mr and Mrs Page's residence…

Sir John Falstaff would eat and drink whenever there was an opportunity, often at the expense of others. He always kept a careful ear to local gossip, and today was no exception. Falstaff was acquainted with Mr Page and his friend Mr Ford and had often heard rumours that the wives held the purse strings to the husbands' fortunes.

Though Falstaff had been accused of poaching, he was a likeable rogue and he managed to wangle an invitation to dine with Mr and Mrs Page, their daughter Anne, Mr and Mrs Ford, and other local dignitaries. During the meal, he thought that Mrs Page and Mrs Ford had taken quite a liking to him, and so he decided that he would win the hearts of the two gentlemen's wives. Once that was done, he would persuade them to share their husbands' money with him. A brilliant idea, thought Falstaff, already planning ways to spend the money. He truly believed that there was no way that any woman could resist his

charms. Making eyes at Mrs Page and Mrs Ford, Falstaff was certain that he had won the hearts of these two reputable ladies.

At the Garter Inn that night…

After dinner, Falstaff joined Nim and Pistol, who were drinking at the Garter Inn, and told them both of his plans to cheat the two ladies of their wealth. 'My honest lads, I will tell you what I am about. I have written a letter to her – and another to Page's wife who couldn't keep her eyes off me either.' Falstaff went on to explain how both women were leering at him during the dinner, and he was certain they could be seduced. 'We will thrive, lads, we will thrive!' Falstaff rejoiced.

Pistol and Nim were rogues indeed, but they considered this silly idea to be too ridiculous. Catching Falstaff completely off guard, both Pistol and Nim refused to take the letters to the ladies, thrusting them back at him. Somewhat surprised by this, Falstaff beckoned his page Robin and told him to deliver

the letters with haste. Extremely angry with his two cronies, Falstaff cursed them both, 'You rogues, begone, vanish like hailstones, go!'

Pistol and Nim, disturbed by the fury of Falstaff's lamentations, decided that they would tell Mr Ford and Mr Page of his plan.

Doctor Caius discovers he has a rival…

Having consulted with his friend Hugh Evans, Slender sent his servant Simple to see Mistress Quickly, who was friendly with Anne Page. Simple gave Mistress Quickly a love letter, which she promised to deliver to Anne. Mistress Quickly worked for a Frenchman named Doctor Caius, who was also in love with Anne.

As the letter was being passed to Mistress Quickly, Doctor Caius arrived. Mistress Quickly urged Simple to hide in the

closet so he would not be detected, for Master Caius was a short-tempered man and would be deeply offended if he were to discover that a letter had been sent to Anne by Slender.

Doctor Caius had come home to get something from his closet and, to his surprise, found young Simple hiding there. The doctor demanded to know what Simple was doing in his closet. Simple told Caius that he had come to deliver a letter for Mistress Anne Page from his master, Abraham Slender. When the doctor heard that the idea had come from Hugh Evans, he decided to challenge Sir Hugh to a duel. How dare he interfere in the doctor's plans to marry Anne!

After Simple and the doctor left the house, Fenton, another admirer of Mistress Anne Page, entered. Fenton was a gentleman and very handsome, and Mistress Quickly promised to help him win Anne's heart as well.

Mrs Page and Mrs Ford compare love letters…

Robin delivered Falstaff's letters to Mrs Page and Mrs Ford, who could not believe the audacity of this over-sized rat of a man. Naturally, they were surprised, even shocked, at receiving such declarations of love from Falstaff. Mrs Page had not the slightest interest in Sir John Falstaff. How could he ever have come to believe that she had designs on him? She wondered what could have made him think that she was attracted to him. After all, he knew that she was married. This kind of behaviour was unwarranted and unforgivable.

When the two ladies compared letters, they found they were identical. They discussed the contents and were certain that Falstaff probably had a thousand letters, most likely all identical, and that he went about trying to make love to every woman he laid eyes upon. Mrs Page could not believe that this fat rogue with a belly the size of Windsor Castle could even think that she would be attracted to him.

Illustration 1. I am Sir John Falstaff

'Let's consult together and punish this rascal,' said Mrs Page with a smile.

Mistress Quickly was also a friend of the two ladies and happened to visit them for their usual tea and chat. All three ladies discussed Falstaff's immoral conduct and got quite excited about recent events. They came up with a plan: Mistress Quickly, chuckling to herself, agreed that she would carry a message to Sir John Falstaff inviting him to Mrs Ford's house.

Mr Ford and Mr Page are told about Sir John's amorous intentions

Pistol and Nim had managed to find Mr Ford, who was, unfortunately, a very jealous man, especially regarding the affairs of his wife. When they told him that Falstaff had made advances to both his wife and to Page's wife, he could hardly believe his ears. Although he assured Pistol and Nim that his

wife would never cheat on him, certain doubts started to unfold in his mind.

Talking to himself, he said, 'I will find this out.'

When the two men had left, an anxious Mr Ford went straight to Mr Page to discuss this most dreadful news. Mr Page was absolutely confident that his wife would never entertain a fellow such as Falstaff.

While Mr Page and Mr Ford were discussing the matter, some friends arrived and told them about Doctor Caius, who had sent Sir Hugh Evans a challenge. However, they said the doctor had been instructed to meet Evans at one place, and Evans had been instructed to meet the doctor at another. This way they would avoid hurting or killing each other. Satisfied that neither Caius nor Evans would ever meet to fight, they all made their way back to the Garter Inn.

Mr Ford comes up with a plan to discover the truth…

Although Mr Page showed little concern about the letter that Falstaff had sent to Mrs Page, Mr Ford had begun to consider ways to spy on his wife. Disguised as a man by the name of Mr Brooke, his plan was to pay Falstaff to arrange a meeting between Mr Brooke and Mrs Ford. This way he would find out whether his wife was being unfaithful to him.

Meanwhile, Falstaff was at the Garter Inn. Pistol, his rascal of a friend, was short of money and had asked Falstaff if he would lend him some. Falstaff's angry words echoed in Pistol's ears: 'You'll not bear a letter for me, you rogue?' In light of Pistol's refusal to carry his letters to the ladies, Falstaff refused to lend him a single penny.

Mistress Quickly came in and asked if Falstaff was anywhere to be found, as she had urgent news for him. 'Sir, here's a woman would speak with you,' said Falstaff's young servant Robin. Mistress Quickly beckoned Falstaff away from his

friends and spoke to him in a quiet voice, saying, 'There is one Mistress Ford, sir, you have brought her into such raptures as 'tis wonderful.' She went on to say that Mrs Ford had many suitors, in fact, so many that she had lost count. There were knights and lords and earls, all begging that they may visit with her. She went on to tell Falstaff – painting such a pleasant image – that Mrs Ford had no interest in these men, who sent letter after letter and gift after gift, for she loved only Falstaff.

'Master Ford, her husband, will be away from home,' confirmed Mistress Quickly in a sincere voice. She then went on to deliver more amorous news, declaring that Mrs Page had also received his letter and she too would like to hear from him. This revelation was most comforting to Sir John, and he courteously thanked Mistress Quickly for her kind deliberations. With this, he set about drinking another large glass of sack. 'Fare thee well, commend me to them both,' Falstaff said as Mistress Quickly left.

This must have been Falstaff's lucky day, for no sooner had he drank his glass of sack than a second one appeared on his table, courtesy of Mr Ford, who entered disguised and calling himself Mr Brooke. Falstaff immediately noticed this well-dressed stranger, but it was Mr Brooke who began talking: 'I have a bag of money here that troubles me,' he explained, offering to pay Falstaff handsomely in return for information about a particular lady. Mr Brooke continued, 'There is a gentlewoman in this town; her husband's name is Ford.'

Falstaff could hardly believe his luck and confirmed that he did indeed know of a woman by that name. Mr Brooke continued to explain that she had been the apple of his eye for a long while. 'I have long loved her,' though, he said, he had hardly dared let anyone know of this secret. Listening with interest, Falstaff inquired as to what purpose he was telling him this story. Mr Brooke offered Falstaff his bag of gold.

'Spend it, spend it, spend more, spend all I have,' insisted

Mr Brooke. He only required one thing from Falstaff. Mr Brooke explained that he so much wanted to meet Mrs Ford. If Falstaff could arrange this meeting, it would be the perfect way for Mr Brooke to seduce her.

Falstaff, more than willing, agreed to this undertaking. Furthermore, to inflate his own self-importance, Falstaff confirmed that Mrs Ford's go-between, Mistress Quickly, had just this moment parted from him and had arranged a meeting at Mr Ford's home while he was away. Inwardly, Mr Ford was surprised by this news and extremely angry but could not allow himself to show it. Instead, he advised Sir John Falstaff that he should be very careful.

All had been arranged, Falstaff duly paid, and Mr Ford would now have to wait to see the outcome. In light of the recent news that Falstaff had already arranged to see her, his jealousy had grown. He said to himself, 'Eleven o'clock the hour, I will prevent this, expose my wife, be revenged on Falstaff and laugh at Page.'

Doctor Caius and Sir Hugh make their peace…

Doctor Caius had arrived at the designated meeting place to fight with Sir Hugh Evans and was furious that Sir Hugh had not arrived to defend his honour. The host of the Garter explained his deception and promised to make them both friends again. 'Shall I lose my doctor?' he said, meaning Caius, and 'Shall I lose my parson?' meaning Sir Hugh. Eventually, the doctor and Sir Hugh agreed to make their peace.

Sir John declares his undying love…

Mrs Page was about to set off in the direction of Mrs Ford's home. Mr Ford happened to be walking by and noticed that she was accompanied by Falstaff's page Robin. In Mr Ford's

Illustration 2.   There is money; spend it, spend it; spend more

mind, this further confirmed that his wife and Mrs Page were both secretly meeting with Falstaff. 'Has Mr Page any brains; has he any eyes?' He was now certain that both ladies were guilty of being unfaithful and decided he would have some sport proving the guilt of these two ladies. 'Our disgraced wives share damnation together.'

He was rather pleased that he had been right in the certainty of their guilt, but was also disturbed that his wife was being unfaithful to him. Seeking out his friends, he asked if any of them would like some fun and invited them to accompany him to his house where they would be entertained in a certain fashion. Only Sir Hugh and Mr Page agreed to go along with him.

By now, Falstaff had arrived at Mrs Ford's. Larger than life, he set about declaring his love for her, proclaiming, 'Have I caught thee, my heavenly jewel?' Falstaff continued his advances to Mrs Ford, telling her how beautiful her eyes were and how he had longed for this day.

Musing upon every detail of Mrs Ford's features, like a young boy who had found his first love, he declared, 'What made me love thee? There's something extraordinary in thee.' Teasing Falstaff, she encouraged his affections and advised Falstaff not to betray her. 'I fear you love Mrs Page,' she said. Falstaff denied that he had any affection for Mrs Page, assuring Mrs Ford, 'But I love thee, none but thee.'

'Mistress Ford, Mistress Ford,' cried Robin as he entered the room, 'Mistress Page is at the door.' Falstaff, upon hearing this confusion, decided to hide and slipped behind a partition in one of the rooms. Once Falstaff was hidden, Mrs Page entered, exclaiming that Mr Ford was about to arrive with all manner of officers and people from Windsor to search for a gentleman that he said was there at this very moment. 'If you have a friend here, convey, convey him out!'

The ladies spoke loud enough for Sir John to hear their story. Certain that this was an unlucky event for himself, Sir John

decided he must flee the vicinity immediately. Clearly shaken and extremely confused by this most disturbing and imminent predicament, Falstaff showed himself to both ladies and declared that he should leave with urgent speed for fear that he would be caught by Mr Ford and his brigade. Mrs Page shrieked at Mrs Ford, 'Defend your reputation or bid farewell to your good life forever.'

What both women did not realise was that Mr Ford was indeed coming to his home with his friends to search for Falstaff.

The two ladies suggested to Falstaff that he hide himself in the laundry basket. The problem was that he was so fat he could hardly squeeze himself in. With the help of Mrs Page, he stuffed his enormous rounded belly into the basket.

At that moment, Mr Ford burst in with his friends, catching them all by surprise and demanding to search the house. Mr Ford asked the two servants where they were taking the basket. 'How now? Whither bear you this?' he inquired. Mrs Ford asked

why he needed to know where the laundry was going, unless of course he wanted to do the washing. Mrs Ford shouted for her two servants to leave immediately and to take the basket to the laundry by the river at Dachet Mead in Windsor.

Mrs Page and Mrs Ford decided that it would be even more humorous if they arranged for Falstaff to meet with them again, giving him more hope that he could still win their hearts. They would then betray him once again! 'Let him be sent for tomorrow at eight o'clock,' said Mrs Page.

Sir John takes a dip in the Thames…

Mr Ford was rather embarrassed by his failure to find Falstaff or any evidence that Falstaff had been to his home. He was ridiculed by his wife, by Mr and Mrs Page and by their friends, so, reluctantly, he apologised to them for his jealous behaviour.

However, in the back of his mind, he was still sure that his wife was being unfaithful.

'Fie, fie, Master Ford, are you not ashamed?' exclaimed Mr Page, who was quite content in his opinion that neither his wife nor Mrs Ford would ever consider being disloyal.

At the river…

Mrs Ford's servants, Robert and John, made their way across the field towards the riverbank, quietly joking to one another about what was about to take place. When they arrived at the river, Falstaff was toppled out of the laundry basket. He tumbled straight into the water, sending a huge wave from one side to the other. As the fat knight headed to the bottom of the Thames, ducks and fish darted and swam about to get out of Falstaff's way but, finally, he started to float to the surface, blowing large bubbles. As he scrambled to the water's edge, both servants burst out laughing. Falstaff had certainly had his fill for the day!

One true love…

Anne and the young Master Fenton were in love with each other but Mr Page refused to allow Fenton to have anything to do with Anne because of his past. Fenton came from a good family, but not so long ago he had squandered much of his money on expensive parties. Because Fenton had spent most of his inherited money, Anne's father believed that he was only interested in the dowry that came with his daughter. Mr Page preferred that his daughter marry Slender, who was rich, and ordered Anne not to see Fenton.

Sir John lets greed get the better of him…

Falstaff had arrived at the Garter Inn, cold and wet after his encounter with the River Thames. He demanded something warm to drink and was muttering away to himself, 'Had I lived to be carried in a basket and be thrown in the Thames?'

As Falstaff warmed himself, Mistress Quickly delivered another urgent message to him. She apologised for the unfortunate event that had ended with him being thrown into the Thames. But all was not lost! Mistress Quickly explained that there was another opportunity to meet Mrs Ford, as her husband was out bird-watching. 'I have had enough of Ford, I have had my bellyful of Ford,' exclaimed Sir John. But Mistress Quickly managed to calm Sir John. Falstaff had an ego as big as his huge belly and, although he was confused, his greed got the better of him and he confirmed that he would meet with Mrs Ford.

Soon after Mistress Quickly had scuttled away, Mr Brooke (who was really Mr Ford in disguise) came in to inquire whether

Illustration 3. So throwing him in the water will do him benefit

Falstaff had seen Mrs Ford, as planned. For perhaps the first time in his life, Falstaff told the truth about the events of that morning. 'You shall hear, Mr Brooke, what I have suffered,' panted Falstaff, as he revealed every detail of his desperate encounter with the two ladies and the soaking he had received in the River Thames.

He went on to explain how he had hidden in the washing basket. He told Mr Brooke how he had quaked with fear lest Mr Ford should demand to see inside the basket and find him there. Falstaff continued to explain that he suffered no less than three deaths: the first was from intolerable fright, the next from being thrown in the basket headfirst, and the third from suffering the unwashed smelly clothes which had been packed so tightly on top of him. Falstaff went on to say that he would have to be thrown into the volcano at Mount Etna before he would give up on Mrs Ford. He then told Mr Brooke that he had just arranged to meet again with her.

This time Mr Ford was certain that he would catch Falstaff in the act, saying, 'He is at my house, he cannot escape me!'

Falstaff has another narrow escape, and Mr Ford and Mr Page are enlightened by their wives…

Falstaff arrived again at Mrs Ford's, whereupon she declared her affections for him in sweet tones. Unsure whether the coast was clear, Sir John inquired with trepidation whether or not Mr Ford was, in fact, away. 'He's bird-watching, sweet Sir John,' answered Mrs Ford. At that very moment, Mrs Page called to Mrs Ford, 'What ho, gossip Ford, what ho.' She had come to warn Mrs Page that Mr Ford was on his way home once again with his friends and was still convinced that his wife was disloyal to him.

'I am undone, the knight is here,' exclaimed Mrs Ford in despair.

'Why then Mrs Ford, you are utterly shamed, and,' she said, pointing to Sir John, 'he's a dead man.'

Falstaff decided that he must get away as quickly as possible. He decided to leave by the same way he had come, but Mr Ford's friends were now guarding the door. Certain that he was in imminent danger of being discovered, Falstaff suggested that he hide in the chimney, the chest, the cupboard, or the vault, anywhere, simply to escape Mr Ford. The ladies would have none of it. Then Mrs Ford remembered that she had an old gown that belonged to her maid's aunt, whom Mr Ford had banned from his home some time ago. Thankfully, she was a rather large lady. Falstaff jumped into the gown and hid upstairs. Mrs Ford then called her servants once again to fill the laundry basket with clothes and have it ready to take away.

Mr Ford burst through the door with all his friends following close behind. Demanding to see what was inside the laundry

basket, he was shocked to find it contained nothing but dirty laundry. Sir Hugh Evans felt sorry for him: 'Master Ford, you must pray and not follow the imaginations of your own heart. This is jealousy.'

Mr Ford began to search the house but could not find Falstaff anywhere. But he did find a fat old woman, whom he began to beat:

'Out of my door, you witch, you rag, you baggage, you polecat.'

As the old woman ran from the house, Sir Hugh remarked, 'By Jeshu, I think the woman is a witch. I like it not when a woman has a great beard.'

Feeling rather humiliated for the second occasion, Mr Ford clung on to what little dignity he had left and continued to insist that he was on Falstaff's trail. His friends, rather bemused at his behaviour and recent events, humoured him a little more and then followed him out of the house back to the Garter Inn.

The two wives thought Falstaff had not quite learned his lesson, so they made plans to humiliate him yet again, but this time they would do it with everyone knowing what was happening. Later, Mrs Page and Mrs Ford told their husbands the truth about recent events, thus settling Mr Ford's jealous mind.

Mr Ford, Mr Page and their wives laughed at how Falstaff had been dunked in the Thames and beaten. Mr Page apologised to his wife for being so foolish as to think she would truly be unfaithful, saying, 'Pardon me, my wife, henceforth do what thou wilt.' Mrs Ford then told them all about their latest scheme…

The legend of Herne the Hunter

There was an old legend about a certain ghost called Herne the Hunter who walked about in Windsor Forest late at night. During winter at midnight, he would circle an old oak tree,

Illustration 4. I like it not when a woman has a great beard

which was said to be a magic tree. He would make such hideous noises and sounds, it was enough to scare anyone half to death. Mrs Ford planned to get Falstaff to dress up in fur and horns and pretend to be Herne the Hunter. Mrs Page's daughter Anne, along with her brother and other children, would dress up like urchins and fairies. They would hide until the stroke of midnight, then everyone would rush out and dance around Falstaff. He would think he was surrounded by ghosts, fairies and goblins, and would be scared out of his wits. They would all pinch him until he promised to be good.

'That will be excellent,' approved Mr Ford.

Inspired by the coming night's conspiracy, Mr Page thought that this might be the perfect opportunity for Anne to steal away with Slender. He ordered Anne to wear a white robe. He would tell Slender that Anne would be in white, and that he should take her by the hand, sneak out and get married as fast as possible. Mrs Page had a similar idea and told her daughter to

dress in green. She planned to tell Doctor Caius to take Anne's hand and lead her away.

Third time lucky?

Having shed the old gown he'd used as a disguise, Falstaff returned to the Garter Inn, hoping for some peace and quiet. He was having a glass of wine when Mistress Quickly arrived for the third time with yet another offer to meet Mrs Ford and Mrs Page.

Said Falstaff, 'I have suffered enough for their sakes.' But the old knight was persuaded yet again to meet them both at midnight, and was told to don the disguise of Herne the Hunter, as this would scare off any unwanted interlopers. Falstaff agreed. 'I hope good luck lies in odd numbers,' he said.

Revelations and blessings…

The arrangements to teach Falstaff a final lesson had been made and while everyone was busy preparing with great excitement for the evening's events, Anne Page had found time to write to Fenton, the man she truly loved. While her father thought she would be running away with Slender, and her mother thought she would be running away with the doctor, Anne was planning to steal away with her one true love, Fenton.

The midnight hour was approaching and Falstaff was now on his way to Windsor Forest, dressed as Herne the Hunter.

'Doctor Caius, my daughter is in green. When you see the opportunity, take her by the hand and away with you to be married,' advised Mrs Page. Mr Page, meanwhile, was telling Slender that his daughter was in white.

Both grooms looked eagerly for Anne.

Mistress Anne entered along with others dressed as fairies and goblins. They had brought lights and tapers and all

Illustration 5. We will do it: let him be sent for tomorrow

manner of toys. Everyone took their place and waited for Falstaff.

'The Windsor bell hath struck twelve; the minute draws on. Now, the hot-blooded gods assist me,' Falstaff assured himself. He arrived at the old oak tree in Windsor Forest, dressed as he was told, with horns on his head. 'I am here a Windsor stag; and the fattest, I think, i'the forest,' he softly chuckled to himself, confident that the moment he'd been waiting for would soon arrive.

'Sir John, art thou there, my deer, my male deer?' teased Mrs Ford. Falstaff confirmed he was indeed there and quietly moved closer to Mrs Ford. They embraced each other under the old oak tree in the moonlight. Falstaff was now sure his wishes would come true. At last, he could speak with Mrs Ford and make plans to cheat her of her husband's fortune. Mrs Ford gently whispered to Falstaff, 'Mistress Page has come with me, Sweetheart.' Falstaff could hardly believe his fortune. Here at

midnight, two ladies had come to be with him. Fortune had indeed smiled upon him.

'Alas, what noise?' asked Mrs Page.

'Fairies, black, grey, green and white, you moonshine revellers, and shades of night,' commanded a mysterious voice.

All the revellers suddenly appeared dressed as fairies and goblins. Surrounding Falstaff, they cried, 'Pinch him, and burn him, and turn him about, 'till candles and starlight and moonshine be out.'

After pinching Falstaff black-and-blue, they decided he had had enough. Mr Ford took off his mask, exclaiming, 'Well, Sir, who's a cuckold now?'

'I do begin to perceive that I am made an ass,' said a humbled Falstaff.

At that moment, Slender came rushing back into the forest, shouting and cursing that he had taken the wrong person to church. He thought Anne was dressed in a white gown, and he

had taken her hand and married her, as instructed. But after the marriage vows, he discovered his bride was a boy! Doctor Caius then entered. He too had married a boy!

Mr and Mrs Page were not so amused when their daughter reappeared and told them that she had married Fenton.

'Hear the truth of it,' demanded Fenton, as he told everyone how much in love they were and that love should be the only reason people marry. Mr and Mrs Page were satisfied with this explanation and blessed them both, saying, 'Heaven give you many, many merry days.'

As for Falstaff, he seemed to have learned his lesson… but no doubt he'd be up to his old tricks before his bruises had had time to fade.

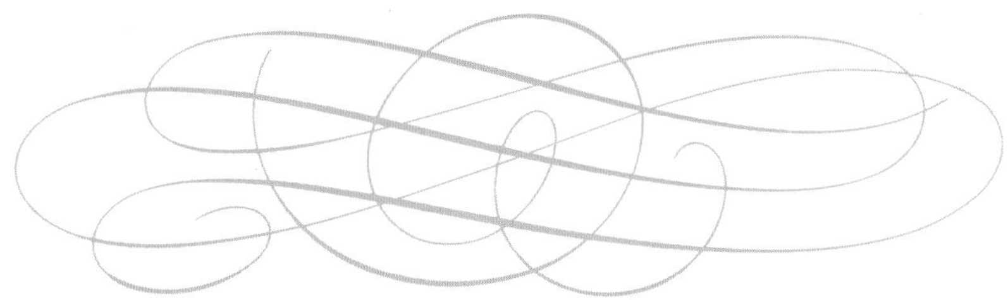

Illustration 6. I am here a Windsor stag

Falstaff

And these are not fairies. By the Lord, I was three or four times in the thought they were not fairies, and yet the guiltiness of my mind, the sudden surprise of my powers, drove the grossness of the foppery into a received belief – in despite of the teeth of all rhyme and reason – that they were fairies. See now how wit may be made a Jack-a-Lent when 'tis upon ill employment!

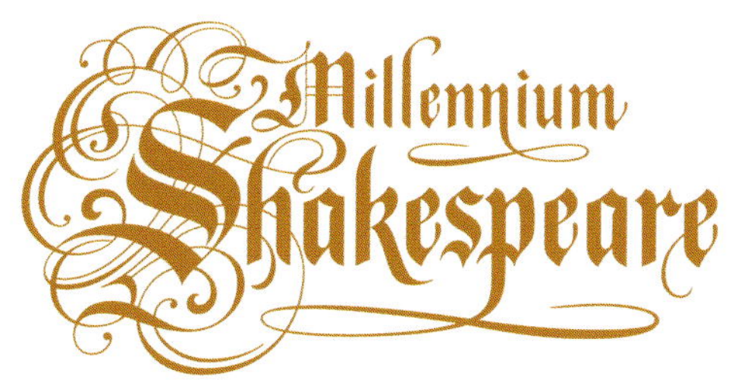

King Lear	Henry V
The Comedy of Errors	Much Ado About Nothing
Titus Andronicus	Julius Caeser
The Taming of the Shrew	Twelfth Night
1 Henry VI	Hamlet
2 Henry VI	Troilus and Cressida
3 Henry VI	All's Well That Ends Well
Richard III	Measure For Measure
Love's Labour's Lost	Othello
The Two Gentlemen of Verona	The Two Noble Kinsmen
A Midsummer Night's Dream	Macbeth
Romeo and Juliet	Antony and Cleopatra
Richard II	Timon of Athens
King John	Pericles, Prince of Tyre
The Merchant of Venice	Coriolanus
Henry IV Part 1	Cymbeline
Henry IV Part 2	The Winter's Tale
The Merry Wives of Windsor	The Tempest
As You Like It	Henry VIII

This is the first series ever published which includes the complete canon of William Shakespeare's works written in modern prose and complemented by works of art.

Copies of all the books in the series are available from the Wine Dark Press Ltd, PO Box 2, Ipswich, Suffolk IP2 0EZ, UK. Alternatively, visit the website below to order online.

www.millenniumshakespeare.com